novum pro

AF010162

Bridie Blackett

Treasured

novum pro

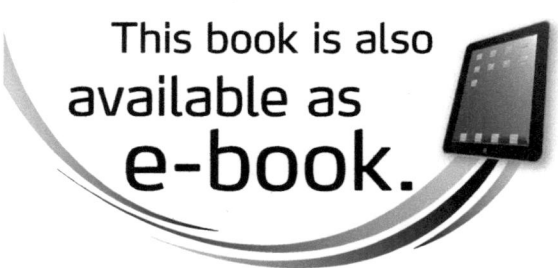

www.novum-publishing.co.uk

© 2016 novum publishing

ISBN 978-3-99048-238-4
Editor: Nicola Ratcliff
Cover photo:
Mauricio Jordan De Souza Coelho | Dreamstime.com
Cover design, layout & typesetting:
novum publishing

www.novum-publishing.co.uk

All rights of distribution, including film, radio, television, photomechanical reproduction, sound carrier, electronic media and reprint in extracts, are reserved.

Printed in the European Union, using environmentally-friendly, chlorine-free and acid-free paper.

CONTENTS

Nana mol 7
My interchangeable family 8
Sleep over 9
Colic 10
Op 11
Hospital 12
Birth of twins 13
Sunday morning 14
Mikki 15
Mollie 16
Newcastle 17
Metro 18
SkinnyPigs 19
Rj's jabs 20
Sleeping baby 21
Miranda 22
Brows 23
Tea 24
Him 25
Tots 26
First time we met 27
Our days 28
Nighmares 29
Stove 30
Weight 31
Leave 32
Grandad 33
Changing 34
Boys 35
Childminder 36

Sicky boy.. 37
Solider boy 38
Secret 39
Trapped... 40
Mol attack 41
Boy with ball.................................... 42
Time goes by.................................... 43
America 44
Mornings 45
Breast feeding 46

NANA MÒL

In and out, that flashy light.
Ne Nor Ne Nor causes a sight.
Calling dad was always bad.
One ring was all it took,
and he was hooked.
Sitting and waiting, letting us in,
Familiar faces do appear.
News we knew came from the crew.
Sad but bright as there's no light.
Days and nights passed too well.
Steroids taken to make her well.
Home bound we go again until,
those pills she takes have no will…

MY INTERCHANGEABLE FAMILY

A house full of kids is all I've known.
Looking for peace, but there is none.
Me and my four, as close as you know.
Different eyes, in and out, short stay, then they go…
Sticking together, through thick and thin.
Not being defeated by whoever comes in.
Trying to break a bond so tight.
Super glue and cement holds us upright.
Fear us not; a kind bunch we are.
Hurt us; be told that you will unfold…
Times move on but we stand still.
Holding the fort but letting you in.

SLEEP OVER

Time has come to let them fly.
Not on their own, but in time.
Spending time at nana's house,
among the fishes, cats and the mouse…
There are dogs so big, standing tall.
May eat my dears is one of my fears.
Chickens they feed over the road.
Walk they will want, but they must hold.
Nana knows what to do, of course she does.
Doesn't stop how I feel, and it never would.

COLIC

Screaming, crying, the whole day long.
Exhausted feelings, ear drum gone.
Walking, jumping, skipping around.
Anything to help the sound.
Demented feeling, unable to cope.
Then tears stop, and feelings get choked.
Time to rest that tired head.
Kettle on, then off to bed.
Eyes closed tight, too tired to fight.
Twin two! Here we go again during the night.

OP

White and bright, clean but mean.
Walking and talking, not too keen.
Hoping, wishing, fingers crossed.
Feelings shattered, as answer is shot.
Wounded and sore, ready to fight.
Next chapter of this tiny life.
Hearts pound so fast, beating away.
Too fast it seems or so they say.
Day is here, I feel the pain.
A tiny hand grips insane.
All breathe is gone I weep with fear.
Oxygen mask on and she is gone…
Seconds, minutes, hours have past.
The longest pain is over at last…
Sleepy weepy squirming around.
Feeling for that tiny hand…

HOSPITAL

Small fragile tiny and weak.
Not ready for air or oxygen to eat.
Beeping and buzzing made time stand still.
Watching helplessly as the crew sorted through.
Naked little bodies just lying there.
Tubes as wire, acting like hair.
Fit in my hand their bodies are still.
Kissing their heads, wiggling to the chill…
Heart pounds fast, knowing they react
Sadness breaks when putting them back…
Caged away in a tiny box
Too early for life so they must fight!
Empty car empty home
Empty beds empty heads…
A mother like me and a father like he
Creates fighters just you wait and see.

BIRTH OF TWINS

So big but too small
As I crawl through the door.
So small to have all
As I squeeze in with all.
They all come together
With help from the crew.
Supportive and strong
As we carry on through.
This journey of ours
Starts in this bed…
Painful but fair
As I push through the chair.
Whipped away at the start
Journey one causes pain.
Number two takes time
Even another day.
Where she appears
Full of life and fears.
Smaller this one as time moves on
A waiting game while they get strong.

SUNDAY MORNING

Pitch black night as day is dawning.
A little noise grows louder and gives warning.
A shiver and sliver in and out,
Hopped in the bed with bottle in mouth.
Twenty minutes or so, if we're lucky at that,
Then the rest appear from the black.
Sleepy and grumpy with tired sore eyes,
Snuggle with us until voices they find.
Needing this and needing that
The morning begins in the pitch dark black.

MIKKI

Whizzing, swooping, flying around,
Jumping, hopping, making sounds.
Watching loving his favourite things
On repeat like his twin.
Long and deep into his soul.
Bares all his thoughts and control.
For those who are dear
He will draw near.
Never alone as he grows,
A shadow is always close.
Lucky he is to have all this.
Lucky I am to have all that.

MOLLIE

Funny, smart and sweet.
Funny, skin deep.
Funny gorgeous girl.
Funny little curls.
Funny from top to toe.
Funniest I've known.
Funny with fun all around.
Funny sounds, giggles and wiggles all around…

NEWCASTLE

Sounds of joy fill the street.
Bag pack on and off to meet
Friends appear full of beer
Ready for the atmosphere.

Racheal Racheal what can I say?
Down in one and she will pay.
Ill to bed not for me she said.
In the chair for more you dare.

Pitta patta Paula here she comes,
Glasses upright, she's ready for the night.
A smile so bright she could give you a fright,
A heart of gold she does hold…

Where is Michelle? She's going to hell
When the lasses get hold she'll be told.

Nichola dear how do you feel?
BAD she said I do feel queer.

Lyndsey the lovely with her future hubby
Rocking and rolling that no single slogan.

Julie Julie dare I say?
How you make me laugh
Whether it's night or day.

Cheers me dears time to rest my head
Thanks for having me again I said.

METRO

Chilly eyes, looking around.
Uncomfortable, nervous, standing their ground.
Light above to secure the pain.
Tracks, in front, are speeding away.
Silent moments, holding your breath.
Looking around, trapped in a nest.
Eyes are distance, some are full,
Others look bare, while others look dull.
Sounds of familiar fill my head.
As I look around and feel the dread.
First time for me this ride of mine,
Accomplished feelings changed my mind.

SKINNYPIGS

Deep, deep breathes in and out
Puffing, panting, passing out.
Lunging deep where no one will go
Pushing the limits destroying the soul.
Bending, stretching, lifting tall,
Shuffling, balancing on the ball.
Heart beating fast and faster still
No breathe to take or even will.
Sweaty, tired, feeling the burn,
Pleasure appears with a gurn…
Exhausting, need to push on through.
Positive vibes feel like glue
holding it together while the weakness passes.
A smile across the faces of those in the classes.

RJ'S JABS

Needy, clingy, attached to the skin,
Can't move too fast or he will win.
Cooking lunch is a flop.
Sandwiches is all they got.
Crying, screaming, shouting on,
Fighting, nipping, all day long…
Visitors cannot believe their eyes
At the amount this boy cries.
Look at him, with that perfect grin.
Makes all the noise just soak in.
Three days of hell to those who know.
Injection time will help him so.

SLEEPING BABY

Creeping, sneaking, slowly in.
Tip toes pointed, breathe held in.
Looking, watching, taking it in.
Pondering, wondering, wanting to get in.
Leaning, turning, twisting around.
Pacing, checking for any sound.
Getting out is harder still.
Use the force and the will.
Hold this moment so very tight.
Until the day he says "night night"…

MIRANDA

Quietly, sweetly, always there.
Opened arms with all the care.
Stranger danger rings in my head.
"Not with this one" a spirit said…
During the night, all things bite.
A ball of safety around us tight.
Nothing can stop the unstoppable.
Nothing would dare, not even you.
A shadow of hope and reality
Comes with this lass, and equality.
No-one different, just the same,
As day is night, and night is day.
We live in a world quite hard at times,
Two breaths of her, and all is hide.

BROWS

Slowly breathing, movements still.
Eyes staring, looking still.
Flicking, twisty turning squeeze
Whatever you do, do not sneeze!
Pulling, plucking, peeling, gone.
Straight and sharp, thin or long?
Brushing, sweeping, gliding lines,
Curving slightly around those eyes.
The moment comes to tell us all
If those brows are there or non?..

TEA

That's three lovely children fast in bed.
Telly is off, I can hear my head.

Tea on the hob… Fizzling away.
Looking around, reflecting the day.

Bobbing and weaving, just getting it right.
Lifting and moving, sorting the night.

There it goes again, that noisy thing.
Demanding of me, not during tea.

Here it comes, crisp and done.
In my belly and gone, gone, gone !

Snugly , huddley, curled up tight…
Ready for the lovelies, and morning light.

HIM

He can fall over those clumsy feet;
Even falling down the street.

Stumbling through the world he goes.
Then he stumbles here, no one knows.

When he stops danger still lurks.
As stopping can then lead to jerks.

Ducking ,diving, dodging that.
O my goodness the poor cat…

Children panic when he's near.
Making noise so he will hear…

Not deaf or daft, this love of mine.
Just clumsy all the time…

TOTS

Running, jumping ,crawling around.
Hopping, lying on the ground…

Bodies everywhere, big and small
Laying, chatting, standing tall…

Confidence grows the longer they wait.
Then time is up and confidence is great.

Brushing through the crowded group,
Following the little one in a loop…

Song time starts; we all sit down.
Listening to words that show us how…

FIRST TIME WE MET

Unusual surroundings I did go
In a room I did not know...

Meeting and greeting those around
Nervous but strong shaking hands...

Fear but fun as I managed on
Until the moment alarm bells rung

Eyes so clear I could not fear
Twinkling stars did appear...

Tasting nerves on my lips
Tingling sensations, how I long for a kiss...

Ties I did but not for long
Ties undone and we move on

OUR DAYS

Let's plan our day and make a tent.
"Don't want that one" the other one said…

Build a robot out of boxes and card.
"No thank you, I'm playing in the yard"…

Let's bake a cake for us to eat.
"Just eaten one thanks cant you see?"

Play doh it is, lets make some shapes.
"No thank you, I'm eating my grapes"

Build the train set and watch it go.
"I've hidden the tracks from my brother you know"

It's time to tidy, the day has gone.
"Let's build a tent, a really big one…"

NIGHMARES

Confused and dazed as the stares give gaze…

Unsure, unaware, understanding the cares…

Feeling undone, defeated under the sun…

Moonlight is bright staring through the night…

Shadows cover the steps in front

Spooking away who ever jumps…

STOVE

Eyes dry, glowing red.
Heat burns in your head.

Sticky, sweaty, dripping down.
Too hot to handle, causing frown.

Cracking, flickering the night away.
Burning bright, keeping awake.

Poking, plunging, shaking around
Ashes all dropping to the ground.

Shining black burnt to white.
Change occurs when ignites.

Peacefully calm, relaxed right through
Muscle melt, calmed with you.

WEIGHT

Mirror, mirror, why me?
Front, back, I can't see…

Hanging over for all to see.
Zip it up, baggy and free.

Suck it in, draw it thin.
Tighter clothes holding it in.

Red or black to hold it back.
Hide away from those who'll laugh.

Sickness forms, stressing self.
Squeezing in that tiny thing.

Scales decided the week before.
Then confront the future more.

LEAVE

Party on before I'm gone
Away to fly really high.

Speeding away on a train track.
No time to be looking back.

Scared happy feelings shot.
Silly line I do hope not.

Learning new courageous ideas.
Folding socks, preventing tears.

Shower fast, water slow.
In and out we must go…

Whoops! My hat! Back upstairs…
"Beret" they shout. God, I'm scared…

Smiley moments do appear
Staring eyes make you fear.

Intimidation is the key
Lock in my hand you will see…

Fears has gone.
I've grown strong
Thank you all as I move on…

GRANDAD

Flat cap set, shoes on tight.
Walking legs ready for the morning bright.

Fells ahead, mind that sheep… it's dead.
Nature has it ways he said.

Cattle grid rattling under our feet.
Cold and ridged, shaking, weak.

Homeward bound, the journey long.
Time passes as we sang songs.

Birds tweeting singing sweet
Fluttering feathers and tiny feet.

Through the window safe eyes watch still
Deciding on the next meal at will.

Sitting there, in his chair.
Eyes close tight and we just stare.

CHANGING

Wiggling, turning, flipping around.
Twisting, sliding, along the ground.

Moving, shuffling, sitting up straight.
On his belly... then his face.

Arms flying, hitting the walls.
Legs fighting the actual cause.

Left undone causes sore bum
Freshened up and he's done.

BOYS

Best friends they are at times they say
Running around fighting their way.

Characters form in those heads of theirs.
Battling it out till the winner fairs.

Running is better said one to the other.
Running is faster do you want to be my brother?

Let's kick the ball around the house.
Don't show mam or she will shout.

Let's plot and plan our adventure together.
Tie up mollie and hide her in the cellar!

Cake is best, it will help me grow.
Big and strong like a GRUFFALO…

Build a den out of sheets all clean.
Mam won't mind! Ssshhh that's mean.

One comes a running the other not far.
Planning their day, having fun they are.

CHILDMINDER

Children laugh and play all day,
Singing songs and painting away.
Stories they tell make us laugh.
The dog and the hog and the bath.

Imagination pours in and out of their heads.
Learning to read, tell tales, and make bread.

Cooking, cleaning, all day long.
Preparing meals from dust 'til dawn.

Play dough set to make a frog.
All along it was a dog…

They teach me things I did not know.
That kings and queens all have moles.

Watching, playing, having fun.
Love my job, if you call it so.

SICKY BOY

Morning breaks and darkness shines.
Noises start. I try to hide…
Twirling, swirling, rolling around.
Deep breathe in, and then he shouts.
Sprays splashed everywhere.
On the chair and in my hair.
Recovering takes a while
Then the boy starts to smile.
Up and out sprouting through.
Again and again 'til he turns blue.
Sleeping long until it's gone.
Chucking up in the middle of his song.
Snuggled in tight but has no bite.
Lifeless and weak with no fight.
Sticky, smelly, sweaty, all round
Shower it is for all in bound.
Everything washed putting germs at bay.
Boy perks up starting to play.

SOLIDER BOY

Age is a number many say.
Youthful advantages have a play.
Travelling along to the unknown.
Misty eyes, afraid and shy.
Proud feelings running through our veins.
Dread and horror causing pains.
New friends appear for a life time long.
Then disappear as time goes on.
The fittest survive the enduring pain.
Time is an enemy, it's all just a game.
Once this passes begin to breathe.
Enjoy the rest of your touring days.

SECRET

Times stands still as I look at you
Others pass by, and I can't bide...
Leaving this place to displace no disgrace.
Quietly goes the secret untold...
Needing wanting you in my arms.
Cannot go to prevent alarms.
Supposition grows for some around.
Don't tell a soul or we will be found.
Clocks ticking fast, time is fun.
Let's tell them all as they should know...

TRAPPED

Tied in knots, scared, still to the bone.
Acceptable in head but feeling alone.
Not close to home so just get on.
Keep it quiet and they'll know none…
Nights are great as darkness falls.
Own thoughts in head beat the dread.
Mornings not bad as I sleep alone.
Work is the best as I smile along.
Need to get strong and find the will.
Something must change and so it will.

MOL ATTACK

Noise so loud hearing through the ground.
Vibrations causing shakes with the sounds.
High pitch piecing notes she hits.
Opera singer, don't get near.
Screaming, crying, like she is attacked.
Jumped out of your skin making you run fast.
Moaning, twisting, groaning on.
Lungs empty but still she's strong.
No idea what brought this on.
As simple as me singing the wrong song.

BOY WITH BALL

Following, chasing, everywhere.
No corners to still as it's not square.
Round and round examined so.
Where will it stop? Nobody knows.
Rolling, flowing, just like a stream.
More than one makes him scream…
Delightful pleasures fill the soul.
Smiles shine as he rolls and rolls.

TIME GOES BY

Most the time motionless.
Wiggle and giggle is the best.
Hands and feet slap the floor.
Crawling now they want more.
Tiny legs muddle along.
Tiny arms as they grow strong...
From a shuffle to a walk.
Next chapter, they will talk.
The moon grows from night to day.
Time passes by, no one will stay...

AMERICA

Hot, sticky, burning air.
Breathing fast to get there.
Back to front all around.
Wrong side up on the ground.
Excited, jumping, feeling high.
Breathe disappears as we fly by.
Queues not long as we carry on.
Imagination is real as to how we feel…
In the movies, part of a play.
Smiling, giggling, what a fun day…
Planning the next thing to do
NASA or Disney? Don't have a clue…

MORNINGS

Eyes tight shut sleeping away.
One eye is opened, little fingers appear…
Knee in spine, foot in mouth.
Whispering words turn to shout.
In they crawl in the warmth of it all.
Chills sneaking in waking us tall.
Up we get as demand is high.
Up and out in the chilly sky.

BREAST FEEDING

Tired, exhausted, feeling drained.
Tiny little one appears from within.
First breathe in, then scream out.
On he goes as he shouts.
Sucking, pulling, latching on.
Satisfaction fills him full until gone.
Painful, sore, tingling away.
Pain and delight for both us this way.
Worth it all, pain does die,
aAs milk coma follows and he rolls his eyes…
Natural and normal for me and him.
Bounding beautifully not making a scene.
Others frown and call us names.
In your face, you bunch of pains.

Rate this book on our website!

www.novum-publishing.co.uk

The author

Bridie Blackett is an up and coming new poet. Treasured, a collection of beautifully written poems, will be her first book. Born in Dryburn, she is 32 years old and a self-employed mother of three. Soon to be married to her fiancé, Rory Red Hodgson, they currently live with their family in Sunderland. As well as writing poetry, Bridie works as a full time child minder. When she does get spare time, she loves keeping fit, eating out and most importantly, spending time with her family.

novum PUBLISHER FOR NEW AUTHORS

The publisher

> **Whoever stops getting better, will in time stop being good.**

This is the motto of novum publishing, and our focus is on finding new manuscripts, publishing them and offering long-term support to the authors.
Our publishing house was founded in 1997, and since then it has become THE expert for new authors and has won numerous awards.

Our editorial team will peruse each manuscript within a few weeks free of charge and without obligation.

You will find more information about
novum publishing and our books on the internet:

www.novum-publishing.co.uk